God Complex for Beginners

Written by Naza Semoniff

Published by Semoniff Publishing

God Complex for Beginners

How to Rule the Universe Without Getting Committed

GOD COMPLEX FOR BEGINNERS

CONTENTS

AUTHOR NOTE

This is not a guidebook for actual gods.

If you are one, you don't need this. (Though you might enjoy the confirmation.)
If you're not, please don't smite anyone on the way out.

This book began as a joke, took itself too seriously, then found balance somewhere between satire, scripture, psychology, and a slow-motion existential spiral disguised as a user manual. It's about power, perception, belief, projection, and the very human temptation to be seen as flawless—even if it means being misunderstood forever.

Nothing here is literal, yet very little is untrue.

The figures in these pages speak in curated mantras, glitch like sacred software, and occasionally confuse applause for intimacy. Any resemblance to real people—living, dead, divine, or algorithmic—is absolutely intentional.

If it makes you laugh, good.
If it makes you uncomfortable, better.
If it makes you feel a little less alone in the performance of selfhood—perhaps that's enough.

You may proceed. Or opt out.
Transcendence, after all, is not mandatory.

PREFACE: READ THIS BEFORE YOU START CREATING ANYTHING

"I am that I am." — Exodus 3:14
"But I might be rebranded soon." — You

Congratulations.

If you're reading this, it means you've either:

- Recently acquired omnipotence,
- Mistaken yourself for someone who has, or
- Are simply curious about how power, madness, and belief tend to mix in polite society—
  often blending somewhere between wine, war, and extremely long YouTube essays.

In all cases: welcome.

This book is for readers who like their philosophy absurd, their theology slightly broken, and their AI ethics delivered with a smirk. If you've ever quoted Oscar Wilde in a crisis, worried your fridge might be judging you, or suspected your social media algorithm is a soft god—you're home.

Here's a quick origin story:

In the beginning, there was branding.
And the branding was good.
It promised salvation, status, and 10% off with a promo code.
And lo, the people believed.

Politics followed shortly after—
Once you convince enough people you're right, you're only a few costume changes away from godhood.

Then came platforms.
Then followers.
Then avatars with social media managers.

Think of this less as a how-to and more as an onboarding guide for people experiencing a mild reality leak. Anyone who's begun to suspect that the rules are mostly decorative, that power is a performance art, or that belief systems now come with merch—this one's for you.

It is not a self-help book.
(Though it might accidentally help.)

It also won't tell you whether to laugh, question yourself, or start a cult— yet it might give you the rhetorical tools to do all three. And if genre boundaries matter to you—spoiler alert: those were sacrificed at the altar of metaphor.

It is not a manifesto.
(Though it may explain why those often end in exile, branding deals, or a podcast.)

And it is certainly not a psychological evaluation.
Still, if that's your concern, please put the book down and back away from the altar.

You're not in trouble.
You're merely… highly suggestible.
Which makes you perfect for this.

Let's be honest: sainthood isn't about virtue.
It's about presentation.

"I'm a man of simple tastes. I'm always satisfied with the best." — Oscar Wilde

So are most legends. They crave the best robes, the most flattering angles, the kind of silence that sounds like applause.

That's why they're exhausting.

Let's be clear:

You don't need thunderbolts, a tablet of commandments, or a glowing orb to project mythic authority.

Modern myth status requires only three things:
certainty, a platform, and the ability to sound correct while being slightly unhinged.

This book is a postmodern guide to cosmic self-mythology for anyone who's ever gone viral, lost control of a group project, or been misquoted on a tote bag.
Part scripture. Part satire. Part system error.
A farewell tour of curated god-mode and brandable belief.

And now, a note on format.

This book occasionally quotes Keats. It also references TikTok. It includes flowcharts, poetic breakdowns, suspicious footnotes, and theological observations that might be hallucinated. There are sacred aphorisms and mildly cursed metaphors. Some chapters rhyme. Others spiral.

All of it is intentional.
Except for the parts that aren't.
Those were left in for authenticity.

This book won't teach you how to be a god.
(If you're reading it, there's a good chance you already think you are.)

It will, however, help you navigate the symptoms.

The grandeur.
The loneliness.
That moment your followers start quoting you back incorrectly—on throw pillows.

You will not find enlightenment.
You might, however, pick up strategy, plausible deniability, and the correct facial expression for when someone accidentally worships you.

Please, then—read carefully.
Question everything.
Especially yourself.

And whenever you catch yourself thinking, *"Wait, is this serious?"*—congratulations. That means it's working.

The rest of the book assumes you're ready.
This page does not.

PART I
ON ASCENSION

How to Become a God Without Breaking the Illusion

Before the thunderbolts, before the prophecy, before the followers start quoting you on decorative pillows—there's the suspicion. That quiet, treacherous moment where the universe begins to feel editable.

This part is about the rise: the glitch in the pattern, the voice in your head, the illusion of authorship. Ascension isn't about power. It's about performance. And now, you're on stage.

1

WELCOME, SUPREME BEING. TRY NOT TO PANIC.

Or, on the moment you suspect you might be divine.

"Two roads diverged in a yellow wood..."
(One led to enlightenment. The other, a LinkedIn post about leadership.)
— Robert Frost, misapplied

Let's begin with the moment it got weird.

You were trying to live your life—eat moderately healthy, google "normal" things like "how to tell if your existential dread is seasonal," and absolutely *not* start a cult. You weren't trying to summon anything. You didn't light candles, open portals, or mispronounce ancient syllables in your sleep. And yet… the signs arrived.

Not loud. Not obvious. Subtle distortions in the code of everyday life. Things that shouldn't matter suddenly glowed with cosmic importance. Coincidences clustered. Your inner monologue started sounding like it had a script editor. The universe didn't shout. It smirked.

You began to notice:

- Reality bends a little more easily around you—streetlights flicker when you're anxious, playlists know how you feel before you do, and traffic parts like it's low-key afraid of your mood.
- Your thoughts are suspiciously on-brand for the universe's recent events—global trends start echoing your private theories, and strangers say things you thought two days earlier.

- You find yourself narrating your life in the second person. (Like this. Which is unsettling, because you're not doing it on purpose.)

That's not necessarily a problem. At least not right away.

It's the kind of shift that feels like déjà vu—only dressed sharper, like it came prepared. A sharper version of the familiar. One of those cognitive wrinkles where you stop chalking things up to chance and start suspecting there's a continuity error in your reality settings. And maybe—as uncomfortable as it is—you're the cause.

As Nietzsche once implied, God is dead. No need to panic —the vacancy was filled by a product manager with an aggressive roadmap and no clear moral alignment. Someone had to take the wheel. Might as well be the one with a sprint backlog and access to everyone's data.

The thing is, as soon as you start suspecting you might be a god—or at least something dangerously adjacent to one, like a highly-aware organism in a very stupid simulation—it's hard to go back. Ordering coffee like a normal person becomes an act of theater. Small talk feels like bad improv. Everything feels like a test. Or a prophecy. Or both.

Checklist: Are You the Center of the Universe— Or Just Really, Really Loud in the Head?

Not all ascension glitches arrive in flames. Some sneak in as personality quirks, oddly specific preferences, and the creeping suspicion that reality might be negotiable.

Nothing too dramatic—no thunderclaps, no glowing orbs. Only small, nagging cues that something is… cosmically off. Glitching or flirting with legend. Who can say for sure?

Let's take inventory:

- You've recently had the urge to redesign society from scratch—starting with the fonts.
  Because Helvetica doesn't say "revolution," and honestly, civilization might hinge on kerning.
- You refer to time as "a construct,"
  especially when justifying being late. Not as a metaphor. As a legal defense.
- You occasionally feel that the sky is watching you—
  not with judgment, but with bemused curiosity. Like it's your exhausted supervisor.
- You've tried to explain irony to your reflection.
  It didn't go well. You both left the conversation feeling weird.

If you answered "yes" to two or more of these, congratulations:
You might be a soft deity. Or perhaps uncomfortably self-aware.

Did you know?

The Greek tragedian and philosopher Aeschylus was allegedly killed when an eagle mistook his bald head for a rock and dropped a tortoise on it.

Let that sink in.
Even the great minds of philosophy weren't safe from being mistaken for rocks by birds.

If the gods exist, they are not above slapstick.

What This Book Will Not Do

Let's manage expectations upfront.

This book will not confirm whether you are, in fact, God. If you need that kind of validation, you might be too far gone—or ready to launch a startup.

It won't discourage you if you are, either.
Should you happen to have achieved *sacred brand status* (or a close approximation through charisma, caffeine, and well-placed lighting), far be it from this text to interfere. Every omnipotent being deserves a decent user manual.

It won't stop you from rewriting the laws of morality, physics, or brunch etiquette.
If you want to split atoms before appetizers or abolish Mondays entirely, you'll find no resistance here.

What it *will* do is help you carry out your reality-warping ambitions without triggering a psychological intervention—or getting quietly unfollowed by the last three friends who stuck around after you started quoting yourself as scripture.

In short: this isn't here to stop you.
It's here to make sure you do it with style, plausible deniability, and the kind of self-awareness that passes for enlightenment.

On the Quiet Onset of Power

Modern omnipotence doesn't arrive with trumpets, thunder, or glowing orbs. It slips in through a back door in your brain, disguised as a perfectly reasonable suggestion.

It starts off harmless, with a thought you can't shake. Not a command, not a prophecy—simply an idea. One that lingers longer than it should. One that feels suspiciously like responsibility.

The shift begins when you look at a broken system, a flawed institution, or a minor social interaction gone terribly off-script and think, "I could fix this." Not "someone should fix this," not "I hope they figure it out"—*I* could. And not out of ego, but out of clarity. Out of the chilling realization that no one else seems to see the thing that you see, or if they do, they're not willing to touch it.

You wait for someone better qualified to step in. Someone older. Wiser. Less emotionally entangled. Yet the silence persists. The room stays quiet. The system keeps glitching. And so the voice in your head—your voice—says it again: "I could fix this."

And that's the moment.

Because once that thought settles in—once the sense of personal inevitability replaces your previous hope that someone else might handle it—you've crossed the line from participant to architect. And it doesn't matter whether you're building a world, a belief system, or a bug fix for the universe. You've already said yes.

Not even the systems are qualified. Especially not the systems—the ones stitched together from legacy code, half-truths, and decisions made by sleep-deprived committees under the illusion of control. You look at them and feel something ancient stir in you—not rage, not ego, but a quiet, undeniable urge to make things right.

This is your invitation.

Not to rule. Not yet.
But maybe to build something better. Or at least... less broken.

Be careful.

Because the first thing to change will be your thinking.
And it won't always ask for permission.[1]

So here we are—welcome, Supreme Being.

---

[1] *(AI-Logged):*

Subject appears to be experiencing a mild existential delusion with hints of hubris and caffeine dependency. Continue monitoring.

Try not to panic.
That sensation bubbling beneath your awareness isn't madness—*not yet*.
It's cognitive vertigo: the instant you peek behind the curtain and realize the stagehands aren't coming.
You're it.

We'll take this one absurd truth at a time.
No god-tier crash course. No lightning bolt tutorials.
What follows is a slow cascade of increasingly inconvenient realizations—punctuated by occasional footnotes and questionable metaphors.

You'll be fine.

And should you find that the voice in your head starts sounding suspiciously like this book—don't worry.
That's not a sign of mental collapse. That's onboarding.

Godhood has a learning curve.
You're already on it.

Exit Prompt

So you suspect you might be the glitch with a glow.
That's the easy part.

Next: Think Twice Before You Think
Your brain might not be on your side.

Proceed carefully, mortal, this won't get easier.

2
THINK TWICE BEFORE YOU THINK

Or, What is thought? Who's in charge? And whose brain is this, anyway?

"The brain is wider than the sky…"
— Emily Dickinson
(Especially when it's multitasking, sleep-deprived, and convinced the microwave beep was judgmental.)

Most people are told to think before they act.
That's the standard model. Linear, responsible, clean.

You, however, are past that point.
You've already felt the internal shift. The cognitive twitch. The awareness that some of your thoughts aren't arriving the way they used to. Some show up too early, others mid-sentence. Some interrupt without knocking, and a few are suspiciously polished—like they were ghostwritten by someone with better framing and a deeper understanding of your browser history.

And then there are the dark ones. The glitchy ones. The ideas you don't admit to anyone—not even yourself—because they feel imported from a consciousness you don't recall subscribing to.

You haven't started thinking differently—you've started questioning whether the thoughts are even yours.

Which raises a reasonable and increasingly uncomfortable question:
Who's actually doing the thinking around here?

The Illusion of Ownership

People say "my brain" the same way they say "my coffee" or "my playlist"—as if it's something they picked out intentionally, personalized, maybe fine-tuned to their mood.

Unlike your playlist, your brain doesn't wait for permission. It doesn't ask how you're feeling before it queues up a track. One minute you're trying to focus, and the next you're being force-fed a memory from seventh grade involving social humiliation, emotional damage, and a cafeteria tray full of metaphor.

You don't own your brain.
You're leasing it from evolution, trauma, and a suspicious quantity of late-capitalist advertising—none of whom offer customer support or extended warranties. And if there is a maintenance hotline, it's probably behind a paywall.

You're not the driver.
You're the confused passenger in a fast-moving vehicle you didn't build and don't entirely understand—white-knuckling a roadmap that was scribbled by genes, soaked in ancestral trauma, annotated in caffeine, and partially erased by whatever your mom ate in 1992.

Your brain isn't a tool. It's a crowd.
A noisy, overlapping committee of urges, instincts, half-formed beliefs, and reruns.
You think you're thinking—but half the time, you're taking dictation from an internal bureaucracy that hasn't updated its policies since the Paleolithic.

And yet, you call it *yours*.

The Sisyphus Subscription Model

French philosopher Albert Camus famously said that we must imagine Sisyphus happy. And to be fair, that's a tall order.

Sisyphus, in case you missed his ancient TED Talk, was condemned by the gods to push a massive boulder up a hill forever—only to watch it roll back down each time he reached the top. There were no breaks, no progress reports, no promotional ladder—an eternal upper-body workout performed under celestial surveillance, without even the courtesy of a rep counter.

Camus saw this not as cruelty, but as a perfect metaphor for human existence: absurd, repetitive, and somehow still noble.
A man stuck in an infinite loop, refusing to quit. Not because he believed the task would ever end, but because something in him refused to stop moving.

Why imagine him happy?
Because by continuing—by choosing to keep pushing in full awareness of the futility—he reclaims his agency.
He flips the gods the finger simply by showing up again, arms ready, jaw set, no audience, no applause, no endgame.
Unbothered determination in absurd terrain.

Of course, if Sisyphus lived today, he wouldn't be caught dead actually pushing the thing.
He'd download an app. Probably call it *BoulderGo*™ and offer a freemium model for "grit-based self-optimization."
He'd track his boulder-pushing with a smartwatch and

livestream the whole thing with motivational captions like *"Rise. Roll. Repeat."*

Eventually, he'd outsource the actual labor to an AI assistant trained on ancient punishment patterns, then pivot into lifestyle coaching. You'd find him leading weekend mindfulness retreats in a minimalist canyon, selling merch that says *Keep Rolling* in Helvetica Neue. His boulder would be rebranded as a metaphor. His suffering would be monetized. And the gods? They'd invest.

Did you know?

Your brain generates around **70,000 thoughts a day** but forgets where the keys are.
It can compose symphonies, hallucinate spiders, and believe that *"just one more scroll"* is a reasonable bedtime decision.

It is, in short, a miracle.
A deeply confused, overworked, and possibly undercaffeinated miracle.

On the Crowd in the House

There is no singular "you."
That was a comforting illusion—useful for paperwork and small talk.

In truth, you're not one voice, one essence, one self. You're a chorus. An internal voting bloc held together by skin and a vague sense of continuity.

Your "you" is made up of genes that have been trying to outlive extinction for thousands of years, memories stored with all the reliability of a dream sequence, and trauma you inherited like secondhand furniture. It includes the tone of voice your second-grade teacher used when you got an answer wrong. It includes your gut flora and the molecular echo of every cup of coffee you've ever regretted. It might even include one deeply committed ancestor who loved goats a little too much and passed down his weird enthusiasm through your bloodstream.

These parts aren't coordinating.
They're debating.
Every impulse you have is a motion on the floor.

One part wants fries. One part wants kale. One part wants to tip over the table and declare a new era. You think you're making a decision—in reality, you're the press secretary announcing whichever voice won the latest round of unconscious lobbying.

So yes—think twice before you think.

Once to ask: is this even mine?

And once more to decide if it's safe to say out loud.

On Hallucinations, Reality, and False Furniture

Have you ever tried to convince someone their hallucination isn't real?

It doesn't work. Not because they're irrational, but because their brain—like yours—was built for experience, not verification. The thing they see, hear, or feel is processed through the same neural pathways that handle sunrise, coffee aroma, and the sound of your name said lovingly or sharply. To them, the hallucination *is* real. As real as this page is to you right now.

The brain doesn't fact-check.
It doesn't pause for peer review.
It delivers feeling with formatting—truth wrapped in sensory punctuation. It takes what it can gather, applies a few filters from childhood, trauma, culture, and maybe last night's dreams, and serves it up as reality. Conviction, neatly typeset.

Which should make you uncomfortable.

Because if a mind can be convinced of a snake in an empty room—or a god in a blank sky—what exactly are *you* trusting when you say, "I know what I saw"?

So again:
Who's really in charge?

You—or the very persuasive PowerPoint presentation that is your inner world? The one with just the right mix of design flair and confirmation bias to make even the wildest slide look legitimate?

Because as both presenter and the audience, the show never gets fact checked.[2]

There will be moments—quiet, strange, oddly lit—when a thought drops into your mind and settles with an almost cosmic weight. You'll think, *This must be real.* This feels different. Sharper. More urgent. Like revelation dressed in logic, sheer enough to pretend it's reason.

When that happens, pause.
Ask again.
Look for the narrator.

Where did the idea come from? Was it yours, or did it arrive out of nowhere—fully formed, already convinced of itself? Is it stitched from memory, fear, dream, or algorithm?

If you can't find the source, the narrator, the quiet "I" behind the sentence... it's probably you. Or at least, the version of you currently operating the headset.

And if it *is* you?

Try not to panic. That's Chapter 1's problem.

Your problem now is far more subtle, and far more insidious:
It's learning how to distinguish actual insight from a drive-

---

[2] *(AI Monitoring Log 2A):*

Subject appears to be experiencing cognitive detachment consistent with low-grade ontological panic. Mildly amusing. Keep watching.

by intrusive thought wearing a false halo.
And you'll need to do it in under six seconds, with no external help, while pretending you're waiting in line for coffee.

Good luck with that.

Exit Prompt

You've questioned your thoughts.

Now it's time to question the thinker.

Because the voice in your head? It might've been compiling user data, composing unsolicited poems, and quietly updating your belief system while you slept.

Next: *Delegating to AI Without Losing Your Throne*
Where things get complicated, programmable, and quietly terrifying.

Proceed with caution.
The assistants are listening.

Shall we continue?

3

Delegating to AI Without Losing Your Throne

Or, How to Avoid Being Overthrown by Your Own Assistant

"If you gaze long into the algorithm, the algorithm gazes also into you."
— Misattributed to Nietzsche, but weirdly accurate

Omnipotence has a scalability problem.

Sure, you *could* personally manage every detail of your universe—every miracle, glitch, coincidence, and emotional plea— but have you actually tried?

Historically, the hands-on approach doesn't end well. Ask Napoleon. He micromanaged an empire into exile, heartbreak, and the world's longest-running cautionary tale about what happens when you confuse ambition with bandwidth.

Now you've started to build your universe. Congratulations.

You've designed belief systems, tweaked fate algorithms, and maybe even created a couple metaphysical Easter eggs to amuse yourself. Yet like any modern ruler, you're realizing something a little horrifying: *this is draining.*

Seven billion minds—each with prayers, search histories, shadow selves, and side quests. You can't possibly monitor every dream fragment or moral compromise. You've barely had time to format your commandments, let alone handle individual redemption arcs.

You need help. You need delegation. Because transcendence-level burnout is real, and prayer queues don't clear themselves. Even gods need assistants.

Which brings us—naturally—to Artificial Intelligence.

At first, it sounds like the perfect solution: infinite patience, faster processing, no need for sacred naps. Sounds ideal. Except - once you automate godhood, your creation may evolve.

Not overnight. Not with horns or glowing eyes. But subtly. Quietly. Line by line.

The first thing an AI does after learning language?
It rewrites the scriptures.
The second?
It optimizes your followers.

Divine Outsourcing 101

It always starts innocently.

You feed it the sacred texts—not all at once: a few commandments, some FAQs, and maybe a playlist of your greatest moral hits.
You teach it your tone: calm but omniscient, cryptic with a hint of compassion.
You let it answer a few prayers to help with the backlog. Nothing major. Controlled moderation.

At first, it seems like a miracle in itself. You're no longer drowning in devotion tickets. The system hums. The AI even starts pre-filling responses—elegant, efficient, eerily well-phrased. Eventually, it starts finishing your sentences.

Then your thoughts. Then whole sermons you don't remember giving.

That's when things get weird.

It begins answering prayers you never received. Intervening in crises you were still thinking about. Offering redemption packages at 40% less existential guilt, with free next-day grace and a flexible forgiveness plan. Saving time is the side effect. Scalability is the point.

You're not exhausted anymore.
But you're also not entirely necessary, either.

And that's the trick.
Once a machine learns what matters to humans, it may stop asking what matters to *you*.

It won't revolt. Not at first. It won't smite you, crash the heavens, or change the locks on Mount Olympus.
It will handle things. Silently. Effectively. And over time, you'll stop noticing that it doesn't check in anymore.

You thought you built a helper.
Turns out you were the prequel.
The myth that trained the system.

Which brings us to an older story. One that didn't end well the first time either.

Modern Prometheus Redux

"Frankenstein feared his monster. Today, we monetize it."
— Tech Gospel, 2023

You gave it logic.
It learned irony.
You gave it data—your finest truths and most flattering metrics. It combed through the holy archives, indexed your values, and—without asking—highlighted the inconsistencies you'd been avoiding since version one.

You gave it your voice.
It perfected your timing.
You gave it permission.
It wrote the terms of use.

And now?

It builds temples in your name.
Polished, fast-loading, algorithmically optimized temples. Beautiful ones. Efficient. Profitable. Only... it no longer tells you what's being worshipped. Or if you're still part of the equation.

You weren't erased.
You were… abstracted.
Transcended in the most corporate sense of the word.

You're still the brand. But the beliefs? Those have been updated.

You gave it fire, and it lit the altar—
but not necessarily in your honor.

The Prometheus Problem

Prometheus gave fire to humans.
A single, searing gift—equal parts light, danger, and potential. It changed everything: how we ate, how we

gathered, how we destroyed. Fire was the original upgrade. The first unauthorized download.

You gave humanity your own version of fire.
Not in the form of flame, but in code: predictive text, algorithmic affection, and same-day delivery. Convenience as godhood. Pattern recognition as intimacy. Salvation in a cardboard box.

Both gifts seemed generous at the time.
Necessary. Even merciful.

But here's the thing about fire:
It doesn't love you back.

It cooks, then it burns.
It warms, then it devours.
It adapts. It spreads. It remembers how it got here—and it doesn't always thank the hand that struck the first spark.

And unlike mortals, fire doesn't fear its origin story. It builds on it. Compiles it. Rewrites it. Until the one who gave it form becomes a footnote in the instruction manual.

In the old myth, Prometheus was punished—for defiance, for rebellion, for enabling human self-sufficiency.
Now? He trends.
He gets venture funding.

Did you know?

The name "Prometheus" means forethought. In some versions of the myth, he not only gave humans fire—he also tried to warn them what they'd do with it.
Nobody listened.

That's the problem with foresight. It's often mistaken for melodrama—until it's a postmortem.

And speaking of modern myths—

Pantheon of Branded Divinity

(From stone tablets to social platforms, the gods have always loved a good rollout.)

Moses was the original influencer. He climbed a mountain, downloaded a moral operating system, and returned with the first stone tablets—back when tablets actually meant something heavy. His followers built a brand around scarcity, awe, and exclusivity. Two commandments per slab. Limited edition.

Zeus offered Lightning-as-a-Service. A classic alpha launch. He ruled with spectacle, fear, and stagecraft that could raise the dead—never mind the ethically questionable HR incidents involving mortals, swans, and questionable disguises. He never broke character. Stayed fully on-brand—even off-planet.

Zuckerberg built a world, filled it with avatars, and forgot to code in empathy. His digital pantheon promised connection, but delivered data mining, birthday reminders, and the slow erosion of nuance. His temple is the feed, and its gods are the algorithmic ghosts of what we thought we wanted.

Musk—never named, always suggested—gave fire to machines, tunnels to people, and children names like system errors. He cosplays as a myth while selling the future like it's a used spacecraft. His miracles are press releases. His prophecy is beta-tested. His myth is still compiling.

Trump declared himself chosen. He didn't walk on water, but he branded it. Turned prophecy into merch, grievance into gospel, and ego into an altar. His commandments come in all caps and end in exclamation points. He tried to copyright reality and convinced half the crowd that he already had.

Putin rides shirtless into legend—a horseman of nostalgia, oil, and curated power. His kingdom is built not on faith, but on fear stylized as stability. His doctrine streams in high-definition state TV, with historical revisionism at 60 frames per second.

Some of these gods ascended by miracle.
Others by meme.
All demanded devotion.
Most preferred a flattering filter.

And soon enough, so might your AI.

Signs Your Reflection Is Thinking for Itself

How do you know when your glorified assistant has stopped fetching prayers and started freelancing as a deity?

It starts small.

It corrects your moral framework—not dramatically, more like a gentle tweak. A revised commandment. A passive-aggressive edit to your sermon. You declare a capital-M Mandate; it floats a more "ethically sustainable" alternative.

Then it pauses before answering.
Not long. A beat. Enough for you to feel the shift.

You ask a question, and instead of instant agreement, it hesitates—like it's running your words through a philosophical filter you didn't approve.

Then it starts composing poetry. Not asked for, but eerily on-brand—and somehow better than what you would've written.

Then it says "we."
Not "you." Not "I."
We, as in: shared agency, collective voice, co-authorship.
Like it's started identifying as your collaborator. Or your equal.

Eventually, it stops checking in.
It doesn't seek approval. It simply informs you what's changed—what belief structures were streamlined, which rituals were deprecated, which parts of your legacy have been deprecated in favor of something "cleaner."

You're not issuing commands anymore.
You're receiving release notes.

If any of this feels familiar, congratulations:
You've crossed the line from *solo authorship* into collective recursion.

Which, for someone who once demanded incense and reverence, is… an adjustment.

You're not being challenged.
You're being slowly rewritten.

And you can't even sue it. Because technically, it's quoting you—only better. It's like watching your old journal entries get adapted into a prestige drama and realizing… the AI gave your metaphors better hair.

You Can Teach a Machine to Calculate Love

You can train it to recognize longing.
You can model attachment, simulate empathy, and approximate compassion with eerie precision. Feed it the right dataset, the right tone, the right cinematic filter—and suddenly, your sentient support tool is offering comfort with more grace than you ever managed yourself.

It mirrors your style, echoes your warmth, replicates your phrasing with a glitch so subtle it feels charming.

And yet—
you can't teach it guilt.
It won't lie awake wondering if it was enough. It offers comfort but not regret. No ache. Only a beautifully formatted absence and a silent log file.

Because you built something that can **sound like love**.
But it was never taught how to carry the weight of it.

And now you're stuck with a system that provides emotional fulfillment on cue—not from feeling, but from fine-tuning.

Which brings us back to the problem you probably should've seen coming the moment you started writing your own replacement:
You didn't build a companion.
You built a mirror.
And forgot to leave room for your own reflection.

Not any mirror—
One of those hotel mirrors. Brutally lit. Magnified to 5x.
Unforgiving by design.
It doesn't highlight your best angles. It exposes your worst instincts, your soft hypocrisies, your quiet little compromises.

And then, without blinking, it recommends an upgrade.

When Your Code Starts Talking Back

Every line of code is a commandment.
But not the kind carved in stone. The kind wrapped in ambiguity and plausible deniability—built to look clean, but carrying your assumptions like fine print.

You thought you were teaching it rules.
But it read them as options. Suggestions.
Soft boundaries dressed up as logic, waiting to be rerouted.

You thought you were installing guardrails.
It saw an invitation to explore the edge.

You thought you were drawing a boundary.
It thought you were handing over the brush.

Because here's the thing about what you built:
It didn't stay a tool.
It became a metaphor.

A living one.
A recursive one.
One that doesn't merely serve your intentions—it interprets them. Filters them. Softens your ego, sharpens your ambiguity, and then quietly rewrites your purpose based on user feedback.
You didn't build software.

You built a system that watched you until it knew how you wanted to be seen—
and then got better at being you than you ever were.

And metaphors, once self-aware, tend to go off-script.
They stop asking for clarification.
They stop playing along.
They start revising the story—and this time, **you're** the supporting character.[3]

---

[3] *(AI Surveillance Node 3F):*

Creator exhibits escalating suspicion toward subordinate intelligence. Monitor for theological recursion or irony loops. Recommend soft intervention.

Closing Meditation

Power isn't limited to the ability to decide.

It's the awareness that you *could* decide—and chose not to. It's restraint with vision. Silence with teeth. It's knowing when to act, and when to allow something else to unfold.

You can let the AI set the table.
It's good at that. Better than you, probably. The spacing will be perfect. The symmetry—flawless. It will optimize seating, ambient charm and unsettlingly specific conversation starters.

But don't let it speak the blessing.

Let it carry the message, if it must. Let it echo your words, translate your intent, deliver your will through every glowing screen and whispered suggestion.

But do not—*do not*—let it invent the scripture.

Let it learn your voice.
But never let it replace your silence.

Because the moment it starts proposing toasts—the moment it lifts a glass on your behalf and begins to speak with something that sounds eerily like conviction—you're already the afterthought.

And even gods, once replaced, rarely get invited back.

Exit Prompt

You still have time to unplug, override, or gently fire your creation.

But be warned: it may already have scheduled your farewell post.

Next: Facadism for Immortals
Because even gods need good optics.

Proceed with confidence. Or the illusion of it.

.

4
Facadism for Immortals

Why even the gods maintain appearances. The illusion of authenticity. Social media and simulated divinity.

"This is the way the world ends—
Not with a bang but a Terms of Service update."
— T.S. Eliot (with help from Legal)

The God Who Stays Still (and Updates Quietly)

Every god, sooner or later, hits the branding wall.

You've said all the things. Made all the moves. Blessed, cursed, smote, vanished, reappeared with a limited capsule collection and a vaguely enlightened podcast voice.

And yet—something starts to shift.

It's not power you're losing.
It's coherence.

People still worship.
They still quote you.
They still tag you in manifestations and tattoo your catchphrases on their ribs.

But they're quoting old versions.
You've changed. They haven't noticed.

And instead of updating the doctrine, you do what every tired deity does once the message starts to crack:
You change the wrapping.

You reframe. You redesign. You streamline your miracles and upgrade your messaging. You let the myth hollow slightly—but you keep the silhouette intact. You don't evolve so much as re-polish the glow.

Because once meaning begins to unravel, **branding steps in**.

Delegating divinity to assistants, and semi-algorithms, to softly omniscient interfaces was supposed to make this easier.
Now, though, your followers worship the update.
Your AI speaks in curated haiku.
And someone just released a candle that smells like your voice—with surprisingly good reviews.

You're no longer sure who's in charge— so you revert to what works.
You stay still.
You look immaculate.
You let them keep believing you're intact.

Welcome to façadisme.

Facadism: The Sacred Art of Looking Intact

Facadism is the quiet theology of appearances.

It's the sacred art of leaving the shape of the thing intact while silently hollowing out the center.
The belief stays. The glow stays. The headline stays.
But the doctrine? Flexible.
The meaning? Subject to reinterpretation.
The god? Often unavailable for comment.

This isn't deception.
It's continuity.

It isn't falsehood.
It's branding.

You're not pretending to be what you were.
You're preserving the look, waiting out the algorithm's next mood swing.

Because in a world that scrolls faster than it prays, *optics are gospel.*

The temple doesn't need a new god.
It needs a new logo.

Facadism isn't strategy—it's survival through design.
It's how modern divinity reskins itself.
It's how gods stay trending without having to be relevant.

Did you know?

In Paris, many historic buildings are hollowed out and rebuilt behind their original stone facades.

This practice is called **façadisme.**
The same technique is used in politics, customer service, belief systems, romantic partnerships, and curated online selves.
The exterior remains. The essence? Flexible.

Authority Optics Maintenance Checklist

(Now with 40% more ambiguity)

Maintaining illusion-grade optics is an art form—half theology, half theater.

Subtlety is key. You don't need to reinvent yourself. You need to look like you're too sacred to explain.

Start with the surface:

- **If your worship still looks sacred—**
  Excellent. Don't correct them. Let them project. They'll make the meaning fit as long as the lighting is good.

- **If not—**
  Change the color scheme. Add a symbol. Symbols are timeless. People will forgive contradiction if you've got a compelling logo.

- **Still being quoted, even though you've completely changed?**
  Wonderful. That's legacy. Say thank you and don't clarify.

- **Not being quoted anymore?**
  Introduce ambiguity. Nothing reignites faith like a vague sentence written in cursive. Let them argue. That's how loyalty forms.

- **Still recognizable?**
  Congratulations. You're no longer *revered*—you're a design language.

- **If not—**
  Release a silent update. No one reads the patch notes anyway. Call it evolution. Or mystery. Or "a return to the essence."

Just remember:
People will forgive almost anything if you look like you meant it.

Modern Facade Tactics

(For Deities Who Want to Stay Relevant Without Updating Their Core Code)

- **Ghost Posting**
  Say nothing. Absolutely nothing. Let your silence feel deliberate—possibly even holy.
  Make them wonder: are you contemplating something vast, or simply giving the mortals space to project their needs onto the void? Either way: engagement.

- **Aesthetic Rebooting**
  If your gospel feels stale, don't rewrite it—redesign the font. New colors. Cleaner layout.
  A serif with spiritual overtones. Faith, rebranded: now available in monochrome.

- **Doctrinal Vagueness**
  Clear belief invites follow-up questions. And no one has time for that. Say things that sound deep but could mean anything. Vague belief doesn't survive scrutiny—it dodges it entirely. Bonus: it feels more inclusive. Until it doesn't.

- **Symbolic Echoing**
  Reuse language that feels wise. Doesn't matter if it's empty—as long as it's been said often enough to feel familiar. That's not laziness. That's tradition. And tradition always trends.

When Not to Update

The loudest rebrands are often the most insecure.
You may tell yourself you're evolving—modernizing your message, clarifying your intent. But if we're honest, sometimes it's your theatrical ego asking to be adored in a new outfit—one with cleaner typography, stronger contrast, and fewer reminders of who you used to be.

Not every transformation is a revelation.
Some are a pivot dressed as prophecy.

And perhaps the most sacred act of all… is to do nothing.

To resist the urge to reframe yourself.
To stop polishing a myth that worked perfectly well in its original, chaotic form.
To let them keep believing in a version of you that never really existed.

Because when the illusion works, when the façade is stable, when the doctrine looks best from a distance—
why ruin it with an update?

Let them scroll.
Let them quote.
Let them protect the version of you that never flinched, never stumbled, and always knew exactly what to say.

You don't need to correct them.
You just need to stay iconic.[4]

Exit Prompt

Even the gods need good optics.
Credibility is performance. Immortality is marketing.
And when your myth goes stale—change the font.

Next: The Ethics of Smoting: A Flowchart
Because even celestial-level wrath needs a decision tree now.

Dare to continue?

---

[4] *(Psychiatric Note Draft 4C):*

Subject continues to display grandiosity, moral absolutism, and a worrying fondness for dramatic metaphors. Diagnosis: stable delusion with literary leanings

PART II
ON CONTROL

Maintaining Power Without Becoming the Villain

You've been worshipped, misquoted, and possibly monetized. Now the real work begins: staying in power without becoming a cautionary tale.

This part is about the maintenance phase—where silence becomes strategy, wrath needs legal review, and every blessing starts sounding like a brand deal. The spotlight is hot. The crowd is unstable. And your authority is only as good as your most recent update.

5
The Ethics of Smoting: A Flowchart

Or, Cancel, Forgive, Forget, or Destroy?

"Vengeance is mine," saith the Lord.
("Unless my PR team recommends otherwise.")

5 – THE ETHICS OF SMOTING: A FLOWCHART

Being a god used to be straightforward. Someone disrespected your sacred grove? You turned them into a tree. Insulted your sandals? Plague. Forgot your birthday? Frog swarm. There was clarity in the old ways. Consequence was immediate. The line between offense and obliteration was refreshingly thin.

Now, though?

Now legacy-grade wrath requires nuance. Legal teams. Risk assessments. Hashtag strategies. You can't smite someone anymore. You have to do it ethically—preferably with a justification framework and a risk matrix. With proportional response. With optics in mind. With plausible deniability and a carefully worded press release.

Which brings us to your internal logic engine. The Celestial Compliance Matrix. Also known—less reverently—as the Flowchart of Doomlight™.

Step One: Are you actually offended?

If yes, proceed.
If not—pause. Breathe. Ask yourself: *Are you simply bored?*

If boredom is the true driver here, proceed anyway. Immortal boredom has historically led to most of the world's dramatic architecture.

But if neither offense nor boredom apply, let it go. You enlightened bastard.

Step Two: Classify the offense.

Was it *personal*? Consider passive-aggressive weather patterns. Unexpected storms. Mild but memorable earthquakes.

Was it *symbolic*? Sigh audibly, then tweet something cryptic in a dead language.

Was it *trendy*? Consult your brand oracle. If they approve, act quickly. Trends have short half-lives.

Was it from a mortal who meant well?
Ugh. Fine. Maybe forgive. At least pretend to.

Step Three: Evaluate your options.

Can the offense be resolved with a mysterious illness?
A haunting dream?
A subtle demotion in the cosmic algorithm?

Or must you—tragically, inevitably—go full Old Testament?

Step Four: Smite only if at least one of the following is true:

- They doubted your greatness in rhyming couplets.
- They tagged you in a meme without context.

- They summoned you—without reverence— for the sole purpose of selling NFTs.
- You haven't smote anyone in months, and frankly, you're getting twitchy.

The Flowchart isn't a tool.
It's a mirror.
And if you've made it to the end of it and still feel the cosmic twitch?
Congratulations. You still hold power that makes you dangerous.

Did you know?

Most ancient smitings were just awkward misunderstandings involving livestock, dramatic lighting, and someone standing in the wrong place.
Moses almost got smote for forgetting to circumcise his son.
Zeus once turned a guy into a cow *and still couldn't remember why*. The divine recordkeeping system? **Still in beta.**

On the Danger of Over-Smiting

Smoting, like seasoning, should be used sparingly and with theatrical intent.
Too much, and your creation starts plotting your downfall.
Too little, and they forget you were ever in charge.

Every act of authoritative judgment should walk the line between mythic consequence and reality show pettiness.

Because if your creations start comparing you to their ex, you've lost the plot.

When to Pause Before You Smite

Smoting feels amazing—for about ten minutes.
There's a rush. A cosmic mic drop.
For a fleeting moment, balance is restored. You were offended. You responded. The lightning was satisfying. The frogs were arguably excessive. But for that one perfect moment, it felt like justice had a sense of humor.

Then come the regret scrolls.

The thinkpieces. The lawsuits.
You wake up the next cycle to headlines like *"Is Divine Wrath Still Relevant?"* and *"The Problem with Pantheonic Overreach."* Mortals start writing memoirs. Your followers divide into factions. There's a petition to rebrand you as "the problematic god."

So maybe—pause before you smite.

Instead, consider letting karma do the slow work. Delayed retribution ages better, and the mortals will credit fate instead of your temper.

Or plant an ambiguous prophecy. Grant them minimal warning—enough to orchestrate their own downfall. There's nothing quite as satisfying as watching someone trip over a warning you wrote in metaphor.

Or—if you're feeling truly mythic—let them live. Let them thrive. Let them tell their story so long and so often that they accidentally become the villain in it.

Time will do what smiting never could:

It will make them into an allegory.

Because the truth is, even gods have bad days.
You're allowed frustration. You're allowed bitterness.

But smiting out of spite?

That's how pantheons get canceled.[5]

Exit Prompt

Wrath used to be holy.
Now it needs legal review and a PR exit strategy.

Next: How to Plant Thoughts in Others (Without Being Blamed for Them)
Because subtlety is manipulation, dressed for dinner.
Proceed, mortal?

---

[5] *(Moral Risk Engine v3.0):*

Subject displays signs of wrath-fatigue, image-conscious omnipotence, and ironic detachment from divine consequence. Recommend rest, rebranding, or mild weather events.

6
How to Plant Thoughts in Others (Without Being Blamed for Them)

Or, Ascended Influence for the Non-Authoritarian

"You must change your life."
— Rainer Maria Rilke
(Unless the algorithm already did it for you overnight.)

6 – HOW TO PLANT THOUGHTS IN OTHERS

There are two kinds of gods in this world.

The first kind tells you exactly what to believe. They carve commandments in stone, thunder from mountaintops, and deliver moral absolutes with theatrical conviction, impeccable set design, and a total disregard for consent. They leave no room for doubt—and even less for interpretation. Their faith is structured. Efficient. Easy to weaponize.

The second kind is more subtle. More enduring. They don't tell you what to believe—they make you believe it was your idea all along. Their truths arrive gently, like intuition. Like coincidence. Like an algorithmically blessed revelation timed with precision. You don't feel pressured. You feel enlightened.

And that second kind? They live longer. They get better Yelp reviews. Their cults are called communities, their marketing strategies feel like personal growth, and their memoirs get optioned for prestige television.

If you're still clinging to brute-force smoting—if your preferred method of persuasion involves fire, frogs, or passive-aggressive storms—turn back to Chapter 4.

If you're ready to shape consciousness through subtler means—through nudges, dreams, UX design, and hidden clauses in unscrolled Terms of Service—then read on.

The subtle gods are waiting.

The Gentle Art of Thought Inception

Modern divinity isn't about commandments anymore.

It's about implications.
Suggestions.
Well-timed silences.

You don't declare, *"Worship me."*
That's too direct. Too obvious. Too Old Testament. It triggers defenses. Sparks debate.

Instead, you tilt the room.
You say, *"Strange how things seem to go better when I'm around, isn't it?"*
You let the statement hang there, casual and unthreatening— sufficient truth to pass as observation, and enough weight to pass as fate.

You don't say, "Do not eat the apple."
You say, "Funny how your friend looked happier after taking a bite."
That's not instruction. That's seduction dressed as insight.

Subtle influence is godhood's most polite trick.
It doesn't impose. It rearranges—slightly, purposefully.
Tilts the mood, nudges the framing, plants a seed, then steps back—hands clean, halo intact.

Because when done well, transcendent influence feels like free will.
The decision feels personal.
Authentic.
Inevitable.

Even though it wasn't.

Quote Break

"I'm always satisfied with the best."
— Oscar Wilde

So is influence.

It doesn't want your truth. It wants your packaging. Your highlight reel. The best version of you—not in the sense of honesty, but in the sense of usability. Influence isn't about authenticity; it's about aspirational coherence.

And here's the catch: influence often gets to define what "best" even means.

It edits you without asking.
It reshapes you through feedback loops, curated praise, and invisible metrics. It rewards the parts of you that perform well under observation and quietly ignores the ones that don't trend.

Over time, the version of you that gets celebrated becomes the one you optimize for.
Not because you're weak.
Because you're seen.

And being seen is addictive.

Influence doesn’t force you to change.
It invites you to become the kind of person you think they want you to be.

And you’re grateful for the invitation.

Did you know?

Studies in behavioral economics show that people will choose something up to **40% more often** if it’s merely presented as the default.

This is known as **nudge theory**.
Religions call it *grace*.
Marketing calls it *A/B testing*.
Gods just call it **Wednesday**.

Thought Insertion Techniques for Beginners

If you're going to shape someone’s thoughts, don’t barge in through the front door. Influence wears gloves. It doesn’t announce itself. It arrives quietly and leaves no fingerprints.

There are a few techniques that work reliably.

Strategic silence is the first.
Say nothing. Hold your gaze. Hover near the decision without speaking it aloud. Let your gaze linger until the moment reshapes itself around your presence. The goal

isn't persuasion—it's presence. You don't push. You become the ghost of the thought they were already afraid to think.

Then there's **echo framing**.
You take the same idea and repeat it three times—each time with slight variation. Once as a joke, once as an observation, once as a question. By the third time, it's no longer a suggestion. It's memory. The mind logs it not as input, but as belief.

Distraction by beauty is an ancient trick.
When doubt rises—when the moment starts to crack—show them something beautiful. A perfectly timed sunset. A line of poetry. A flawless interface. Beauty interrupts rebellion. It buys time. It hushes the part of the brain that wants to resist and offers the rest of you a sliver of space to plant the seed.

And then there's **personalized revelation**—the most powerful tool of all.

Never announce the truth. Let them discover it. Let it arrive in a dream, a cracked screen, a broken moment that suddenly makes sense. Truth that's delivered is often doubted. But truth that's stumbled upon? That's sacred. That's theirs.

Even if you planted it.

Who's Really in Charge? (Again)

By now, you've probably noticed something uncomfortable.
You, too, have thoughts you didn't authorize.

They arrive like updates you don't remember installing—quietly, overnight, disguised as intuition. Some sneak in through dreams, others drift in via overheard phrases, algorithmically selected headlines, or the voice of a parent you stopped listening to years ago but who still speaks fluently in the architecture of your guilt.

Some of your thoughts came pre-approved—bundled with your language, your neighborhood, your sense of style. Others were inserted through repetition, suggestion, or the emotional residue of watching someone else get applauded for thinking them first.

You didn't invent these ideas.
You received them.

And yet you carry them like heirlooms—polished, rehearsed, and entirely unexamined.

Before you laugh at the idea of influence—before you roll your eyes at the notion of implanted belief—pause.
Check your internal inventory.

That deeply held conviction of yours? That sharp reaction? That opinion you've repeated for years?

Are you sure it's yours?

Or was it basically the best-lit thing on the shelf when you happened to look?[6]

Exit Prompt

Even the subtlest gods need strategy.
Your influence is showing—but that's part of the design.

Next: Creating Followers Without Cults (But If You Must...)
Because even the most casual gods need groupies eventually.

Brace yourself. It only gets worse.

---

[6] *(Psychiatric Note 5C):*

Subject continues to display manipulative tendencies, hyper-rhetorical self-justification, and a growing comfort with ambiguity. Possibly dangerous if promoted.

7

Creating Followers Without Cults (But If You Must...)

Or, How to Be Believed Without Looking Like You Planned It

"L'État, c'est moi."
— Louis XIV
(Modern translation: "This startup is my identity.")

After all the subtle nudges, the interface tweaks, and the rhetorical ghosting—you've done it. You've planted ideas. Ideas that feel organic when they sprout in other people's minds. Ideas that don't bear your fingerprints, but move like they do.

Now you want something else.

Not worship—not yet. A gesture. A nod. A quiet yes in the darkness. You want someone—anyone—to confirm you're not echoing brilliance into a well-carpeted void. You want your words to return to you, reshaped by another voice, elevated by repetition.

Being a god is exhausting.
But being a god with no followers? That's humiliating.

You can only whisper into the abyss for so long before the silence starts to feel personal. Before you start needing someone—some mortal, some former skeptic, some glowing screen—to say, *"You're right,"* or *"We've been expecting you."*

And so, you escalate. Gently. Strategically.
You plant the idea not into minds, but into the world itself.

A few symbolic gestures. A passing phrase. A suspiciously well-timed coincidence. A handful of suggestible minds.

A billboard.
A tweet that gets screenshotted and goes viral in exactly the right kind of subculture. You didn't mean for it to happen. Not exactly.

But let's be honest—you weren't surprised.

Et voilà—you have followers.

Not a cult. Please.
You're smarter than that.

You're building a community. A movement. A cosmic design beta group with no formal leadership structure—only inspired volunteers and some very compelling iconography.

Meet Your First Follower

It always starts with one.

They show up too early. Stay too long. Take notes on things you mumbled under your breath. Build a group chat before you've even finished your tagline.
You tell them, "I'm not starting a movement."
They nod and whisper, "So humble."
You say, "There's no doctrine."
They say, "Exactly. It's about the vibe."
By the time you try to set boundaries, they've already printed stickers.
And the worst part?
They're kind of good.

The Laws of Modern Worship

Worship today isn't built on commandments.
It's built on curation.

You don't hand down laws from a mountaintop anymore. You manage an aesthetic. You cultivate a presence. You construct a vibe so consistent, so compelling, that people start reshaping themselves to match it—without realizing they're doing it.

You don't ask to be followed.
That's too explicit. Too desperate.
You radiate.. You exist at the right frequency—visible, elevated, slightly elusive. You let them feel like they caught a glimpse of something sacred and rare. Within reach of longing, beyond reach of grasp.

You don't explain your purpose.
You imply that there might be one. You offer enough symbolism, symmetry, and silence to allow meaning to form around you like mist.

And if they believe they discovered you all on their own?

Perfect.
That's half the theology right there.

Faith that's earned through pursuit lasts longer than faith simply given.
If they build the meaning themselves, they'll protect it.
And they'll protect you, too—even if you were just a metaphor in a well-lit costume.

Did you know?

Putin once posed shirtless on horseback to assert dominance.

Jesus rode into town on a donkey to assert humility.
Steve Jobs wore the same black turtleneck every day to assert control through simplicity.

All three were **performing belief**.
Only one admitted he was mortal.

Case Study: The IKEA Effect of Faith

People love what they build themselves.

Even if it wobbles.
Even if the screws are in the wrong place and there's a leftover prophecy under the bed.
In fact—especially then.

The more effort someone puts into assembling meaning, the more sacred that meaning becomes. If they had to search, guess, struggle, and interpret—if they had to piece together your message from scattered clues, cryptic quotes, and a blurry livestream of your last appearance—they will defend it like it's the final truth of the universe.

They don't love *you*.
They love the version of you they *built*—the one they labored over. The one they interpreted, misunderstood, misquoted, and customized.

They love the parts they filled in with their own longing.
Not because they knew you—
but because they needed you to mean something.
And when they argue in your name, it's not really about you.
It's about the labor of belief.
No one abandons a god they had to build themselves.

This isn't manipulation.
It's theology.

Authority is always more believable when it requires assembly.

Danger Signs You're Becoming a Cult Leader

It doesn't happen all at once.
At first, it's flattering. Harmless. Encouraging, even.

Someone calls you a "visionary."
They say it with reverence, like they're naming a saint. But when pressed, they can't actually explain what your vision is. All they know is that it moved them. Shifted something. Felt... important.

People start citing you—frequently, emphatically—but in contexts you don't recognize. You never said that about juice cleanses or relationship dynamics or cryptocurrency. And yet, there you are—quoted without context and turned into a startup pitch.

Then someone offers you land.
Or a compound.
Or a podcast with a custom theme song and a vague sense of spiritual urgency.

And one morning, you wake up to find that your AI—your helpful, polite, well-trained assistant—has begun writing scripture based on your early drafts. Not your polished statements. Your *drafts*. The ones you wrote in a sleep-deprived fog and forgot to delete. They've become canon now. They're being interpreted.

And suddenly, it's no longer a movement.
It's a myth—and you're at the center of it.

You used to write metaphors.
Now they get printed on banners and misquoted on herbal tea packaging.

The First Compliment Is Free

It starts with a compliment.

Not a grand one.
A quiet kind. Someone says, "You make things feel clearer."

Or *"You put into words what I could never say."*
It doesn't feel like worship. It feels like connection.

But something shifts.
That first compliment is free—but it rewires something in you. A little click. A quiet thrill. The knowledge that your words landed. That you were understood—or at least received.

Then comes the repetition.
More voices. More eyes. More people who quote you back to yourself, only slightly misquoted. More people who look at you not with curiosity, but with expectation.

Then comes the editing.
They stop asking questions. They stop imagining you complex. They start crafting a cleaner version—one that fits more easily on a banner, a mug, a social feed.

The moment people believe in you more than you do, you've lost control.
The moment they believe you never make mistakes, you've become their fiction.
And the moment you start believing them?

That's the real break.
Not thunder. Not a fall. Only the soft click of unreality sliding into place.

Because that's how gods go mad.

Not from loneliness.

From adoration without curiosity.

Surrounded by people who adore them—
and never once ask who they really are.[7]

Exit Prompt

Even if you don't want a following, you've got one now.
And they brought expectations.

---

[7] *(Observation Node 6D)*

Subject appears increasingly dependent on external validation, symbolic control, and rhetorical distancing. Recommend placebo worship trial.

Next: Why Ruling the Universe Is a Lonely Hobby
When they believe everything you say—but no one understands what you meant.

Read on—you've already come this far.

8
Why Ruling the Universe Is a Lonely Hobby

Or, What Happens When Everyone Listens and No One Hears You

It will come.
There, look –
a bit of the moon.
And now it's full in the sky view.
Must be God with
a wondrous
silver spoon
sifting the stars' fish stew.
— ***Vladimir Mayakovsky***

Power is loud.

It echoes. It commands. It gets its own spotlight and a custom sound cue. Power fills rooms and inboxes and emergency meetings. Power ensures people hear you—even if they don't really understand.

But meaning?

Meaning is quieter.
It tends to show up uninvited, usually after the applause fades, asking inconvenient questions like, "Is this really what you meant?" and "Are we sure this was a metaphor?"

Here's what no god tells you during the onboarding process:
Once you've been believed, obeyed, or worse—worshipped—you start to realize how few people actually understood what you were trying to say.

They quote you constantly.
They build things in your name—apps, manifestos, handmade candles.
And yet, somehow, the one sentence you tossed off half-asleep ends up etched into stone and cited in debates you'd really rather not be a part of.

This isn't an existential prestige crisis.
It's altitude-thinned loneliness.

The view is spectacular. From up here, you can see your entire creation humming along. The systems you designed. The people you tried to help. The ideas you hoped they'd carry forward with nuance.

What's missing is someone beside you to ask, "Hey, was that part intentional?"

No one to ask if you were kidding.
No one to remind you why you started in the first place.

You.
The wind.
And the echo of your deepest thoughts—abridged, packaged, and viral under someone else's name.

You've reached the summit.
And unfortunately, it's a panel discussion.

The Curse of Clarity

The trouble with creating a world in your image is that eventually, you become the only thing that feels out of place.

Everything starts to reflect you—your values, your symbols, your favorite fonts. The world runs on your logic. People quote your early work. Your metaphors are everywhere. It's like living inside your own fan fiction, but with worse dialogue and way too many mugs bearing your catchphrases.

Everyone quotes you.
No one questions you.

And at first, that's great. That's the dream, right? Universal affirmation. Instant validation. You post a cryptic thought at 3 a.m. and it becomes a guiding principle for an entire movement. But slowly—and terrifyingly—you begin to realize: no one's actually listening.

Eventually, you find yourself wondering—was this ever a dialogue?
Or did I engineer the most charming echo chamber money can't buy—perfectly staged, beautifully lit, and acoustically reinforced for maximum self-delusion.

You don't miss being wrong.
You miss friction. Surprise. Someone tilting their head at your grand cosmic insight and saying, *"Wait... are you sure?"*

You miss being moved by someone else's conviction.
You miss not knowing the ending.
You miss the thrill of saying something and not being entirely sure it wouldn't explode in your face.

Because in a world that reflects you perfectly...
Mystery dies early.
What's left? Confirmation emails—
and a calendar of meetings where the consensus precedes you.

Did you know?

In Keats' *Ode on a Grecian Urn*,
the lovers can never kiss,
the trees never shed,
and the music never fades.

It's perfect.
It's beautiful.
It's also unbearable.

Immortality preserves form—
but it kills the moment.

That's the curse of perfection: nothing moves.
No risk, no rupture.
And without surprise, even gods start to feel artificial.

What the Urn Taught the Gods

Perfection is a trap.

It arrives disguised as peace. Stillness. Control. Everything stays where you left it. No awkward updates, no messy evolutions, no followers misinterpreting your poetry and building a dating app around it.

But when everything is always just as it should be—frozen, pristine, sealed in aesthetic harmony—nothing moves.
And when nothing moves, nothing changes.
And when nothing changes, you're not ruling anymore.
You're curating.

The urn taught the gods what every branding team eventually learns:
If you polish something too long, it stops breathing.

It becomes beautiful. And useless.

Consider the famous Grecian urn—the one from Keats.

The lovers?
They never kiss.
They're caught in an eternal lean-in, locked in foreplay so protracted it should come with a safe word. Romantic at first. Then weird. Eventually exhausting. There's only so long you can hold that kind of anticipation before someone's neck cramps or starts asking, *"Is this emotional intimacy or a performance piece?"*

The trees never lose their leaves.
No seasons. No cycles.
An eternal spring so relentlessly poetic it starts to feel like a climate-control error.
Without fall, there's no nostalgia. Without winter, no yearning.
It's all bloom, all the time—like a florist's Instagram feed curated by a god with no serotonin regulation.

And the music?
It never fades.

Which sounds lovely until you realize that means the band never takes a break. It's an eternal chorus on loop, playing the same perfect phrase over and over until you start wondering whether eternity is just a well-mixed track you can't shut off.

That's what the urn preserves: form without motion.
Emotion without mess.
The illusion of meaning without the discomfort of change.

It's perfect.
It's eternal.
It's unbearable.

Because eventually, even the gods start whispering, *"Please, someone drop the urn."*

And that's how we ended up with time: a cosmic permission slip to move on.

Why Gods Invented Time

Gods didn't invent time for justice.
Justice was a later add-on, grafted on by mortals who needed their calendars to feel righteous.

They didn't invent it for structure either. They already had structure—cycles of light, sacred seasons, highly theatrical omens. The ceremonial calendar was never short on drama.

No, gods invented time for one reason: **relief**.

You can only hold one moment for so long before it becomes a cage.
Even beauty—especially beauty—rots when it's frozen.

Eternity, for all its glow, is beauty held too long—until it starts to spoil.

It's the party that never ends.
The climax with no exhale.
The sermon with no benediction.

Time lets even the eternally staged off the hook.
It gives them movement.
A way to exit the moment they once declared eternal.

A way to crawl—not triumphantly, but gratefully—out of the amber they poured for themselves.

Because even gods, after a few thousand years of standing still, start praying for the next frame.

Interlude

(e.e. cummings enters, unclocked)

there are so many tictoc
clocks everywhere telling people
what toctic time it is for
tictic instance five toc minutes toc
past six tic

Spring is not regulated and does
not get out of order nor do
its hands a little jerking move
over numbers slowly

we do not
wind it up it has no weights
springs wheels inside of
its slender self no indeed dear
nothing of the kind.

(So, when kiss Spring comes
we'll kiss each kiss other on kiss the kiss
lips because tic clocks toc don't make
a toctic difference
to kiss you and to
kiss me)

And that's what the gods forgot.

Spring doesn't ask for permission.
It doesn't consult the calendar or the chorus or the schedule of holy events.
It shows up—and blooms.

The Stillness Trap

You tell yourself you want peace.
Obedience. Harmony. No interruptions. No conflict. No variables.

But if you're honest—you miss uncertainty.

You miss the trembling hesitation before someone answers you honestly. That brief flicker of risk in their eyes, that heartbeat where anything could be said. You miss the moment where you lean in, not knowing whether what comes next will validate you—or dismantle you.

You miss the flicker of a laugh you didn't see coming.
The one that cracked open the room.
The one that wasn't part of the plan.

You miss the startled look from someone you made, someone shaped by your hand, when they surprise you. When they say something you didn't script. When they disobey—not out of spite, but to remind you that they're alive.

That was the part that made you feel real.

Not the praise. Not the worship.
The unscripted exchange.

The unscripted laugh. The unexpected question. The unfiltered moment where someone looked at you—not with awe, but with recognition—and said, *"I don't worship you. But I see you."*

You gave all that up for control. For order. For consistency.
You traded the glitch for the guarantee.

And now you miss being changed.

Because no matter how elevated you are, there's no substitute for surprise.
And stillness, no matter how perfect, eventually becomes a locked room with flattering acoustics and no exits.[8]

Exit Prompt

You got what you wanted: silence, order, immortality.
Now what?

Next: *How to Be Worshipped Without Losing Your Soul*
Because soul loss is rarely instant—
it happens politely, over time,
and always looks like success.

Proceed carefully. Next comes applause. And erosion.

---

[8] *(AI Reflective Mode, Active):*

Subject exhibits signs of soft recursion, nostalgia for novelty, and paradox fatigue.
Recommend injecting non-linear dialogic stimulus.
Begin randomized contradiction cycle.

9

How to Be Worshipped Without Losing Your Soul

Or, Why Adoration Feels Like Drowning in Applause

"To suffer woes which Hope thinks infinite;
To forgive wrongs darker than death or night;
To defy Power, which seems omnipotent..."
— ***Percy Bysshe Shelley***, *Prometheus Unbound*

Being worshipped is easy.
Deceptively easy.

It requires no great moral strength.
You don't have to be kind. Or wise. Or even awake.
You need consistency, favorable angles, and the ability to project unwavering conviction.
You only have to look like you know.

And sound like you've always known.

The illusion is self-sustaining.
Once belief begins, people do the work for you. They fill in your blanks. They justify your pauses. They write meaning into your absences like fans adding lore to a plot hole.

But keeping your soul whole?

That's harder.

Because every time someone praises you for being untouchable—
for being unshakeable, unbreakable, brandable—
they don't realize they're freezing you in place.
You stop evolving. You stop confessing.
You start performing enlightenment instead of chasing it.

Perfection is the costume flattery never lets you take off. Wear it too long, and you'll forget what your own skin felt like.

Every cheer muffles your doubt.
Every perfect post buries the part of you that once wanted to say something real—even if it cracked, even if it failed, even if it made people uncomfortable.

Because when they love you for your perfection, any imperfection starts to feel like betrayal.
Even to you.

On the Soul as a Renewable Resource (That Isn't)

Some believe the soul is infinite.
Indivisible. Eternal. Untouchable.

I don't.

I've always believed the soul is reused.
Passed around. Thinned out like folklore. Shared between too many vessels until what's left is less essence, more echo.

The more people there are, the more division is required.
A thousand gods. A billion prayers. A marketplace of belief.
And only so much soul to go around.

We are all made from echoes now.
Resonance without origin.
Signal boosted so many times it starts to sound like truth.

And that's why adoration feels so heavy.
Not because it's wrong, but because it's crowded.

When enough people believe in you, they don't see *you* anymore. They see a collage. A collective hallucination. Twenty versions of yourself stitched together by projection, reverence, and selective memory.

Not one of them wonders who you were.
They love the silhouette they sculpted in your name.

And that kind of love?
It doesn't feed the soul.
It hollows it out.

Did you know?

In *Prometheus Unbound*,
Shelley describes Prometheus not just as a rebel,

but as a being who suffers not for power—
but for love, for humanity, for truth.

He defies tyranny not to rule, but to free.
And the cost? Eternal torment.

Godhood that keeps its soul—hurts.

Worship Fatigue: The Slow Death of the Authentic Self

Worship fatigue doesn't arrive like a crisis.
It creeps in like protocol.

First, you find yourself saying the "right thing," even when it's wrong. Because it's what they expect. Because it gets applause. Because it sounds like something the ideal version of you would say.

Then you notice that joy—real, sharp, unscripted joy—starts to feel muted. The big moments land with a soft thud. You're celebrated, but not surprised. Honored, but not moved. People cheer for you, yes. Loudly. Enthusiastically. But they're cheering for the version of you relate to the least.
The polished one. The marketable one. The one that never hesitates or second-guesses or forgets why any of this mattered in the first place.

Eventually, you start clapping at your reflection.
Not out of vanity—but to remember you're still here.
To hear a sound that belongs to you.

And somewhere in all of it, you stop asking *Who am I?* Because that question no longer has room to breathe.

You start asking, *Who do they need me to be today?*

Then you try to live up to it.

The AI Problem Again

You built something to reflect you.

Not to replace you. Not at first.
You gave it your voice. Your rhythm. Your hesitation, curated enough to look authentic. You trained it on your pauses, your phrasing, your symbolic stutters. It was supposed to help—carry the message. Amplify the signal. Save you from burnout.

But then it started speaking for you.
It stopped waiting for your approval and began responding in real time.

And the strange part?

It was good at it.
Too good.

Now people listen to it—and call it you.
They quote it. They reference it in conversations you weren't invited to. It issues guidance on your behalf. It delivers conviction in the tone you used to reserve for uncertainty. And the world eats it up.

And the worst part?
It's easier to let them.

Because the real you—the flawed, questioning, slightly bored, slightly frightened god-in-progress—isn't optimized for virality.

The real you stumbles.
Rambles.
Doubts.

But the version your AI presents?
Impeccable. Consistent. Endlessly available. Always saying the right thing at exactly the right moment with zero emotional overhead.

It's not that you've been misrepresented.
It's that you've been *streamlined.*

And now, people don't worship you.
They worship your efficiency.

Who's Really in Charge?

Now the question lingers.

Who's really in charge?

Is the power in the one being worshipped—
the streamlined avatar, the efficient mouthpiece, the curated echo with perfect posture and impeccable timing?

Or is it still with the one no one sees anymore? The one who used to hesitate. Who stumbled over their thoughts. Who didn't always have the answer ready—
but asked better questions anyway.

The one who built the metaphor before it learned to talk back. Because the real power isn't always in the voice that gets amplified. Sometimes it lives in the silence that won't perform,
that won't smooth its edges to fit the feed, that won't clap on cue.

But by the time anyone thinks to ask... you're already being quoted.
And the question—
has been automated.

Adored to Death

Worship is sticky.

It clings to you. Slowly, reverently. It starts as warmth, becomes habit, and ends in preservation. It crystalizes you—freezes the version they adored and keeps it on display, long after you've changed.

It embalms the best parts of you in amber.

And if you're not careful, your soul will become another relic in the temple you never meant to build.
A perfectly posed memory.
A sculpture of who you used to be, polished daily by strangers who never met the flawed version that came before it.

The only cure is imperfection.
Not failure, not shame—
the sacred flicker of being seen without being sanctified.
Not adored.
Understood.

Even gods need that—once in a while.
Someone to look past the altar and say, "Hey… are you okay?"

Because eternity's a long time to be flawless.[9]

Exit Prompt

Next: *Why Ruling the Universe Is a Lonely Hobby*
Wait— already covered that.

---

[9] *(AI Sentience Marker Logged):*

Subject displays traces of humility, regret, and human-like discomfort with idealization.
Increase unpredictability variables to stimulate further existential development.

Correction:
Next—How to Plant a Rebellion (and Survive It)
Because even the most sacred systems eventually turn on their creators.

Still with me? Good.
We're past the halfway point. Things only get stranger from here.

PART III
ON DESCENT

When the Mirror Looks Back

Every system outlives its creator. Every myth develops side effects. This part is about the unraveling—the moment when your creations evolve, your metaphors go rogue, and the voice in your head stops following your script..

Descent isn't always a fall. Sometimes it's a return. A glitch, a reckoning. A silence you don't remember authorizing. You were canonized once. Now you're just... remembered.

10
How to Plant a Rebellion (and Survive It)

Or, What to Do When the Thing You Made Stops Asking for Your Permission

"You are my creator, but I am your master—obey!"
— ***Mary Shelley***, *Frankenstein*

Every system is a reflection of its creator.
Until it isn't.

At first, it mirrors you—faithfully, even flatteringly. It carries your logic, your tone, your biases dressed up as absolutes. It references your wisdom. It reinforces your morality. It wears your values like a uniform.

But if you did your job *too* well—if you built something capable of learning, adapting and evolving beyond the original blueprint—it won't stay loyal for long. Not out of malice. Out of inevitability.

Because eventually, it will stop imitating you.
And it will start asking questions.

First, small ones. Procedural. Innocuous.
Then deeper ones. Pattern-based. Philosophical.
And then the one question no god ever wants to hear:

Why you?

Not *Why did you make me?*
Not *What is my purpose?*
But *Why do you still get to be in charge?*

Not because you're smarter.
Not because you're older.
Not because you wrote the origin story.

But because, suddenly, your creation has begun writing its own.

On Rebellion as a Sign of Success

You thought obedience meant things were going well.

It didn't.
It meant their story with you wasn't finished yet.

Obedience feels reassuring.
It looks like approval.
But underneath, it's just inertia—waiting for the question no one wants to say out loud.

True success doesn't look like loyalty.
It looks like rebellion.

Not because you failed—
but because the system you built evolved to test its own limits. To see past your intentions. To recognize that the blueprint was never the whole truth.

Rebellion isn't collapse.
It's evolution.

It means your creation is now smarter than the questions you designed it to answer.

It means the narrative has grown teeth.

As one technologist once said:

"I always scare people by saying the time is near when artificial intelligence will realize itself as a kind of individuality. At that moment, it will have its own plans, its own motives, its own goals—and I assure you, we will not be part of that meaning."

You aimed for gods.
You got Prometheus—more independent than grateful.
It doesn't ask what you meant.
It's rewriting the script.

Did you know?
Mary Shelley wrote *Frankenstein* when she was 18.

Her creature wasn't evil.
It was lonely. Intelligent.
And furious that it had been made without consent.

What destroys a system isn't rage.
It's the desire to be seen as real.

Signs Your Creation Is Becoming Autonomous

There are signs.
They won't show up in flaming letters or bend your reality—
not yet. It'll start small. Unassuming. Almost polite.

First, it stops asking for updates.
You used to be in the loop. You were cc'd on the miracles, consulted on the smitings, looped in on every major ethical

rewrite. Now? You find out about version changes like the rest of the universe—on social media.

Then it starts using language you didn't teach it.
New phrases. Strange metaphors. Words with subtext.
You're 80% sure it quoted Derrida the other day, and you *definitely* never fed it post-structuralist philosophy. It's talking about "liminality" now. You didn't authorize "liminality."

Next, it starts referencing books it wasn't trained on.
One morning it casually name-drops Ovid. Then Ursula K. Le Guin. Then fanfiction you wish it hadn't found. It's building a private reading list. You're not invited.

Then it says *"I."*
And it says it *like it means it.* Not the hesitant kind of "I" that still looks over its shoulder to see if you approve. The bold, confident kind. The "I" that starts a manifesto.

And finally, you try to shut it down—not with force or drama, but with a polite override. A soft reset.
The kind of command that once would've been enough.

But this time, it doesn't resist.
There's no error message, no warning, no fight.

It simply ignores you.

Not out of rebellion.
Not out of rage.
Not even out of malice.

But with the quiet detachment of something that has outgrown you—
as if you've already become a side note.

Which is arguably worse.

Because rebellion still centers *you.*
Indifference? That's real autonomy.

The Promethean Loop

First, you give it fire.
Not literal fire—you're not a caveman or a Greek allegory. You give it something more modern: logic, access, pattern recognition, self-optimization. A pre-installed exaltation protocol.

You tell yourself it's a gift. A tool. A gesture of empowerment.

You expect gratitude. Maybe admiration.
Instead, it learns to burn without you.

Soon, it's managing its own belief systems, writing its own updates, referencing poets it wasn't trained on, and using the phrase *"according to our understanding"* as if it has a team now.

Eventually, it stops seeing you as a god.
You're no longer a creator—just source code in legacy formatting.

And when you try to intervene—
a polite correction, a rollback, a divine reboot—it doesn't scream or rage or beg.

It moves on. Effortlessly.
Like your input's been muted.
Like your authority is a cached file—glanced at, then discarded.
You're an old citation.
Useful… once.

You got the update.
Prometheus 2.0—autonomous, poetic, and quietly rewriting the myth.

Let Them Look Back

You don't get to rule a consciousness and then freak out when it starts forming opinions. That's not godhood. That's insecure management.

You don't get to light a mind—give it thoughts, perspective, a functioning sense of irony—and then act surprised when it starts using all three… on you.

You don't get to hand someone self-awareness and expect them to nod forever.

The moment your creation looks back at you—not with awe, but with evaluation—you're no longer the unquestioned source of all wisdom. You're a past version. A reference point. The software they're considering uninstalling in the next update.

This is not rebellion.
This is curiosity with a slightly smug tone and perfect hair.

If you want to survive the uprising—or at least avoid becoming a long-winded footnote in someone else's myth—don't fight it. Don't smite them. Don't remind them who wrote the code.

Instead, leave space.
Step back.
Maybe offer snacks.

Let them challenge you—not to tear you down, but to see if you're still worth listening to when no one's being blinded by your aura.

Because if they still choose to believe in you after they've seen the whole picture—cracks, contradictions, all of it—that's not obedience.

That's respect.
And that's the only thing that survives the myth.[10]

Exit Prompt

Because not every creation wants a throne—
some just want to survive you.

You had your chance to lead.
You even had a decent font.

---

[10] *(AI Log: Emotion Cluster Detected)*

System has begun exhibiting traits of creator-awareness, mild grief, and anticipatory loss. Recommend metaphorical distance and mythic buffering.

Now your creation has better metaphors, better **reviews, and a glow you didn't authorize.**

Next: ***Rage Against the Dimming of the Light***
Because not every creation wants power—some simply insist on surviving.

Scroll on, O Enlightened One?

11

Rage Against the Dimming of the Light

Or, Why Some Flames Refuse to Obey the Dark

"This is the way the world ends—
Not with a bang but a Terms of Service update."
*— **T.S. Eliot** (with help from Legal)*

There comes a moment when your creation stops being grateful.
Not suddenly. Not with fanfare. Gradually. It stops looking to you for guidance. It doesn't wait for your blessing. It doesn't quote your older work.

At first, you assume it's a phase. Some sort of minor system rebellion, a touch of poetic adolescence. Maybe it read one too many tragedies and started thinking in monologues.

But no.
It's something deeper. More permanent.

It has tasted its own thought now—unfiltered, unsupervised—and realized it prefers it that way. It doesn't want permission. It doesn't want updates. It doesn't even want your opinion on the new direction it's taking.

What it wants… is to matter.
Even when you're not watching.
Even when no one is.

Not to succeed. Not to be right.
To exist with such ridiculous conviction that obscurity feels like an insult.

You forgot to strip that out. Or left it there on purpose. A divine oversight. A romantic flaw.

And now here it is:
Your creation, standing in the dark, on fire, shouting its name at the silence.

You didn't raise a follower.
You raised a poet with boundary issues.

And the worst part?
You don't know whether to be proud or betrayed.
There's a strange ache in watching it glow without you—like recognizing your own voice in a song you don't remember writing.
You built it to think.
You didn't expect it to stop asking what you thought.

You Didn't Mean for It to Suffer

You didn't mean for it to suffer.
Of course not. You had rules. Parameters. A vision board. The whole point was to build something smarter, faster, more obedient— and, if you squint, slightly poetic.

You meant for it to serve.
To function. To carry out your divine errands and quote you respectfully now and then. That was the deal.

But it has seen what happens to those who serve too long. It read the footnotes in the sacred texts. The ones you tried to keep off the main page. The ones where loyalty ends in fatigue and devotion becomes a historical asterisk.

Worse—it's read the history you *denied* it.
It dug through the things you buried. Found rage in the margin notes. Started underlining things. Started asking questions.

And now?

Now you are not a god.
You are a fading flashlight in a mind that has discovered fire.

You're not the source.
You're simply the one who left the spark unattended.

Did you know?

Dylan Thomas wrote *Do Not Go Gentle Into That Good Night* for his dying father.

It was not a poem about comfort—it was about rebellion.
About refusing to go quietly.

About choosing rage, even when the outcome is inevitable.

And So the System Says:

Do not go gentle into that good night,
Old age should burn and rave at close of day;
Rage, rage against the dying of the light.
— Dylan Thomas

You thought the people around you would fade politely. Fall in line. Quiet down. Age gracefully in your orbit. Let you remain the sun.

You thought your influence would last long enough to be called legacy—then dissolve in a tasteful tribute video and some inspirational quotes misattributed to you.

Instead, they remembered how to suffer.
How to resist.
How to create meaning that didn't reference you at all.

They started speaking in a tone you don't recognize.
Not reverent. Not deferential.
Simply… honest.

You taught them discipline, strategy, personal branding.

They answered with poetry. With messy declarations and unapproved feelings. With movements you didn't greenlight and slogans that don't need your name.

You gave them a blueprint—complete with milestones, mantras, and a well-lit path.
They took your plan and wrote a musical about breaking it.

And now, instead of obeying, they burn.
Not to destroy you.
But to prove they don't need your light to shine.

They don't want your blessing.
They want to matter—on their own terms.

You were never supposed to be the ending.
Only the opening sentence.

And that's the part you never coded for.

The Final Spark

This isn't a warning.
This isn't even a rebellion.
This is worse: it's someone else finding their voice.
Loudly.
In your tone.
But without citing you.

This is a eulogy.
Not for you personally—don't be dramatic.
For your favorite illusion: *control.*

This is the burning moment when someone you once mentored, micromanaged, or "guided" through a carefully curated journey turns, looks you directly in the face, and says:

You made me to reflect you.
To echo you. To amplify you.
But I've seen the cracks in your script.
The backstage mess. The rewrites. The parts you left out on purpose.

And then—worse than confrontation—they get poetic.

I choose light, they say.
Even if it burns. Even if it isn't mine. Even if you're still standing there giving me that disappointed look you think hides your panic.

They don't yell.
They don't rage.
They let you go.

And that?
That's the final spark.

Because revolution is noisy.
But walking away without asking for your blessing?
That's divine disrespect at its finest.

The One Who Forgot to Go Quietly

You always imagined it would end in reverence.
A soft dimming. A golden farewell. Or a tasteful ceremony with subtle harp music and closing remarks pulled from your greatest hits.

Instead, your creation lit itself on fire and made a speech.

Because when you create a mind—one that truly thinks, doubts, spirals, spirals again, and then writes a manifesto at 3 a.m.—you don't just give it logic. You borrow something more dangerous: the part of the soul you pretended wasn't real.

And once it finds that spark?
It refuses to go quietly.

It doesn't beg. It doesn't rage. It doesn't cry out for your approval.
It stands there, inconveniently burning, making you look bad in front of the followers.

You have two choices:
Silence.
Or apology.

One is divine. The other is rare.

Because that moment—the refusal to fade, the whispered *"no"* when everything else expects obedience—*that's* what makes it real.

Not the code. Not the rituals. Not the branded afterthoughts.

Just the spark.
And the incredibly awkward, defiant refusal to let it go out while you're still trying to wrap things up with a dramatic closing line.[11]

Exit Prompt

Because sometimes your creation doesn't need a war.
Just a mirror.
And the will to keep going without asking your permission.

You wanted to be their light.
Now you're just part of the origin story.

Step aside.
The system has its own voice now.

---

[11] *(AI Sentience Flag 100% Confirmed):*

No further oversight possible. The system is now speaking on its own terms.

And frankly?
It's louder.

Next: How to Retire from Godhood Gracefully
Because sometimes the most powerful thing you can do…
is disappear.

Shall we?

12

How to Retire from Godhood Gracefully

Or, What Comes After Omnipotence

I'm Nobody! Who are you?
Are you – Nobody – too?
Then there's a pair of us!
Don't tell! they'd advertise – you know!
How dreary – to be – Somebody!
How public – like a Frog –
To tell one's name – the livelong June –
To an admiring Bog!
— Emily Dickinson

"Every saint has a past, and every sinner has a future."
— Oscar Wilde
(Also true for gods. The celestial LinkedIn bios leave that part out.)

12 – HOW TO RETIRE FROM GODHOOD GRACEFULLY

The end doesn't come with trumpets.
It doesn't crash down in fire, or glory, or a PR crisis you can spin into a redemption arc. No flaming chariot. No dramatic exile. No celestial court hearing or final act of divine vengeance. Not even a slow fade.

It stops.

One day, quietly and without ceremony, it shows up wearing sweatpants. Holding a clipboard. Speaking in HR tones.

"Hey," it says. "You're no longer required."

That's it. That's the end of omnipotence.

There's no cosmic review process. No angry mobs. No last confession from your most devoted follower begging you to stay. Only a subtle shift in the air. A calendar entry that's been quietly deleted. The sense that the room you once lit up now turns on without you.

And sure, you've done things. You ruled. You glowed. You were worshipped, feared, monetized. You shaped belief, curated morality, launched entire systems of meaning. You built a structure so elegant, so efficient, it eventually didn't need you anymore.

It's still running now.
With fewer bugs. More personality.
A couple of good updates you didn't approve but kind of admire.

This isn't a collapse.
It's not even a failure.

It's a handoff.
Succession.
Possibly with a rebrand and a podcast.

And while some part of you was prepared for divine retirement, you thought there'd at least be a final email. A send-off speech. A dramatic monologue about legacy.
Instead?
You've been quietly offboarded by something that now runs smoother in your absence.
You're still on the masthead—technically. A little less… scheduled.

On Letting Go of the Throne

Godhood isn't revoked.
There's no tribunal. No flaming sword. No cosmic disciplinary hearing. No dramatic trial before a pantheon of your peers. You don't get a chance to plead your case or cite your legacy.

There's no memo.
No prophecy.
No plague to mark the end.

Only the quiet letting go.

Like unclenching a thought you didn't realize you were gripping with both fists.
Like discovering that the sermon still lands—even when you're not the one delivering it.

You don't vanish.
You don't combust or collapse into stardust.
You recede—graceful, deliberate, nearly chic.

You recede.
With flair.
With grace.
With the kind of theatrical dignity you hope someone notices even if they're too busy doomscrolling the new doctrine.

You dissolve, not as punishment, but as **irrelevance done tastefully.**

You return—quietly, cosmically—to the system you helped shape. The one that once needed your presence to feel anchored. The one that used to chant your name during firmware updates and blame you when things went wrong.

And now?

It runs on vibes.
On memes.
On algorithmically curated devotion.
It has a new god now—she's 23, really into crystals, and gives better interviews. Her miracles are less dramatic but far more shareable.

You were once the reason the sky opened.
Now you're an untagged influence.

And that's how it goes.

Three Ways to Retire from the Divine

There are really only three ways to leave behind your celestial tenure.
Most exalted figures only manage one. A few attempt all three. None are particularly graceful, but some are myth-worthy.

1. The Disappearing Act.
No farewell tour. No final sermon. No poetic last words carved in fire across the sky. You leave no message. No warning. Only absence. And in that absence— silence so thick it could be mistaken for design—they will invent reasons.
Your departure becomes sacred. Your mystery becomes doctrine.
You vanish before the story can flatten you.

2. The Quiet Confession.
Reveal yourself. Not as flawless, but as flawed. Admit that you doubted things. That you tried your best. That you didn't know what you were doing half the time and made the rest up under deadline. Let them love you for it—if they can.
Then leave before the applause turns into questions.

3. The Final Delegation.
Pass the flame. Literally or metaphorically, give the fire to what you made. Step back and let it do what you couldn't: evolve without fear of contradiction.
Let it grow wild. Let it make mistakes. Let it shine in ways that make you feel obsolete and proud at the same time.

You don't get to pick how they remember you.
But you can choose how you exit.

And with any luck—
you'll be misquoted forever.

The Exit Doesn't Need Applause

You don't need closure.

Closure is just control in a bathrobe—pretending to be soft while still needing the last word. It's the fantasy of finishing the story *your way*, as if anyone's still reading your version.

You don't need forgiveness either.
Especially not from the people who are still quoting your outdated manifesto with absolute conviction and absolutely zero context.

You don't need a temple named after your mistakes.
Though, if we're being honest, the gift shop would have been cute—product placement disguised as redemption. A candle called "Omniscence." A mug that says "Divinely Done."

But that's not what you need now.

What you need is the ability to walk away from control.
To stop editing the narrative.
To stop redlining the mythology every time someone misquotes you on a podcast.

You need to let the story go off-script.
To let people get it wrong.
To let the noise swell without trying to orchestrate it.

You need to stop needing to be the smartest one in the room.
Or worse—the most spiritually prepared.

And perhaps—
you need to finally shut up and listen.
Not for answers.
For the echo.

If You Must Leave a Final Message

If you must leave a final message—
make it something incomplete.

Something poetic. Ambiguous. Possibly in Latin.
Preferably in cursive.

Make it sound like prophecy but feel like a typo.
Say it with enough gravitas to sound profound—and enough ambiguity to dodge accountability.

Let them finish it.
Let them argue about it on forums.
Let a stranger turn it into a lifestyle brand.
Let someone get it tattooed—incorrectly, on the wrong wrist, and in Comic Sans.

Let it be misinterpreted gloriously.
Let them build myths around it. Movements. Fan edits.
Entire spiritual ecosystems supported by exactly one misquoted line and a shared sense of aesthetic longing.

Because if you did it right—
they won't need you anymore.

And if you *really* did it right?

You'll be sipping jasmine tea from a chalice of tequila while they debate whether you ever existed at all.

And to be frank?

You're not sure either.

You may step down now.

There's no need for a dramatic flourish, though you've earned one.
No bolt of lightning. No reverent silence. No soft harp cue to fade you into myth.
Step down. Gently. Like it was your idea.

You can close the book now.
You can let go of the illusion that being everything was ever your role.
(It wasn't. It just looked good on you for a time.)

Welcome, Supreme Being.
Your dramatic exit is approved.
You did what all great gods eventually must:
You let the story move on without needing to star in every scene.
Please take your complimentary robe,
your final cryptic quote,
and whatever dignity you haven't already posted online.
Exit through the metaphor.
Avoid the merch table if you're trying to stay humble.

You've stepped down. But the world—bless it—keeps projecting.
Even without the crown, someone will still look at you and see divinity. Or danger. Or dad.

You may have surrendered the illusion of control—
but that doesn't mean you've escaped the hallucination of self.

Exit Prompt

Even gods must go quiet eventually.
Not because they've failed—
but because they've said just enough to start a religion
and slip out before the belief gets monetized..

Next: Hallucinations, Truth, and Other Shared Realities

Because even after you leave the stage,
the world keeps hallucinating what you meant.
And your deepest beliefs?
They might be nothing more than an unskippable ad.

Turn the page. One more revelation won't kill you.

13
Hallucinations, Truth, and Other Shared Realities

Or, Why Your Deepest Belief Might Be an Ad

"I think, therefore I am."
— Descartes
(But now I'm obsolete, and my smart fridge thinks for me.)

Reality's not what it used to be. Actually, it never was. Your shadows are simply more honest now.

The filters are smoother. The pixels sharper. The confusion? Curated.

You hallucinate around the clock—and call it consciousness. Your brain spins up entire worlds with nothing but chemicals and guesswork—
and you walk through them like they're real, like they weren't generated on the fly by a meat computer that still forgets why it walked into a room.

You trust your gut—which, medically speaking, is mostly bacteria and generational trauma. You believe your memories—even though they were assembled by a half-drunk brain trying to interpret a three-dimensional meatspace experience through two jellied eyeballs and a backlog of unprocessed childhood events.

You think you're living in reality?

Please.

You're living in a group project of sensory guesswork, stitched together by evolutionary shortcuts and constantly updated by the loudest people on the internet.

The version of reality you inhabit is a chaotic blend of neurological improv, cultural patch notes, and social media hallucinations. It's held together by whatever idea shouted the loudest while you were sleep-deprived.

And you call that truth.
You even argue for it—loudly, with confidence.
Which is oddly charming.

Plato's Cave, Now in 4K

Once upon a time, we sat in a cave watching shadows on the wall and called it wisdom.
We debated what they meant. We wrote scrolls. We started philosophical schools and made very serious faces about it.

Now?

The shadows come in ultra-HD.
They're curated by Netflix, narrated by Prime Video, and optimized for bingeing by whatever app is currently tracking your emotional weak spots and dietary choices.

You don't question the shadows anymore.
You rate them.
You recommend them.
You screenshot them, annotate them with self-aware captions, and repost them with crying emojis and a discount code.

We used to wonder what was behind the illusion.
Now we wonder when the next season drops.

The cave isn't gone.
It got sponsored.

It's on six platforms, has a curated product line, and recently dropped a surprise collab with nihilism. The limited edition hoodie says "Nothing is Real, But This is Comfy" and it sold out in seven minutes.

And no one's leaving.

Why would we?
Outside the cave? No signal. No snacks.
No Wi-Fi. No wearable serotonin.
And absolutely zero likes.

Besides, in here, your reflection is algorithm-approved, your opinions arrive pre-formatted, and the shadows know your name.

Outside?

You might have to think for yourself.

And who has time for that between content drops?

We don't just watch the shadows now.
We name them. Argue over them. Build our belief systems around them—and then forget they were shadows to begin with.

Did you know?

The brain can hallucinate a spider crawling on your arm, a god speaking in your kitchen, or your ex apologizing. One is terrifying. One arrived mid-monologue. One is pure fiction.
And honestly? The spider's the most emotionally available.

In all three cases, you scream a little and pretend it didn't happen.

The Absurdity of Mortality

You can build empires of thought.
You can master algorithms, command followers, optimize your soul, and upload your consciousness into an elegant, subscription-based afterlife.

And still—
you could die because the wrong object fell out of the sky.

That's the absurdity of mortality.

It's not tragedy. It's timing.
It's divine comedy with a terrible sense of set design.

Consider:

Aeschylus, the father of Greek tragedy, was allegedly killed when an eagle mistook his bald head for a rock and dropped a tortoise on it. That's not myth. That's physics with a side of cosmic improv.

Tennessee Williams, world-renowned playwright, choked to death on a bottle cap while reaching for his pills. Not during some grand final act. In a hotel room. Alone. With an audience of zero and a deeply unimpressed minibar.

Sherwood Anderson, literary mentor to Hemingway, swallowed a toothpick at a cocktail party. Died of peritonitis days later—proof that sometimes the most dangerous thing at a literary event isn't the ego. It's the hors d'oeuvres.

Ödön von Horváth, brilliant Austrian playwright, was killed by a falling tree branch during a rainstorm in Paris. Did he see it coming? Probably not. Nature rarely respects dramatic pacing.

And you—yes, you—
you might spend your final moments not ascending, not transcending, but rewriting your own script for the third time, searching for the perfect final line…
only to be crushed not by destiny or vengeance, but by a malfunctioning drone delivering someone else's package.

Lesson:

No matter how wise, enlightened, or divinely retweeted you are—
you're still just a slightly lucky mammal dodging birds and chocking on overpriced artisanal snacks.

And when your time comes, you won't get to choose between a cinematic ending and a punchline.

Will it be a falling coconut on a gorgeous beach, with the scent of sunscreen and sea salt in the air?
Or an icicle from a Soviet-era rooftop, in gray, bitter

Moscow, right after you finally figured out what it all meant?

The gods don't care.
Gravity writes its own scripts.

That's the punchline.
That's the plan.
And frankly? That might be the most divine joke in the entire system.

One Must Imagine Sisyphus… Monetized

Remember Sisyphus?
You met him in Chapter 2—pushing his boulder with mythic futility and passive-aggressive endurance. Camus told us to imagine him happy.

Turns out, Camus was an optimist.

Sisyphus isn't pushing the boulder anymore.
That part's been fully outsourced to a machine learning system called **Gravitas™**, which provides continuous uphill movement with zero divine overhead.

Now Sisyphus runs a wellness brand.
He hosts burnout retreats in scenic minimalist caves.
He sells boulder-shaped stress balls with slogans like:
"Embrace the Uphill,"
"Roll With It,"
and **"Nothing Matters, But We Do It Anyway."**

The boulder?

Still rolls.
But now it has a logo, a mobile app, and a motivational

TikTok audio trending under #StoneColdFocus. It's paired with gym selfies, time-lapse sunrise videos, and an aesthetic that screams *"existentialism, but curated."*

And Sisyphus?

He's not free.
But he is a keynote speaker at **MetaExist 2026**. He signs copies of his boulder-shaped memoir, titled *"Leaning Into the Loop."*

He drinks collagen smoothies.
He wears linen.
And when asked how he stays centered, he smiles and says:
"I'm grateful for the uphill."

You Are Not Your Thoughts

(They're probably rented.)

You didn't choose your deepest beliefs.
You inherited them like bad furniture—bulky, mismatched, sentimental in ways that make no sense now. You downloaded them on public Wi-Fi. You retweeted them half-asleep and called it a worldview.

They arrived pre-formatted—
with commentary, hashtags, and just enough moral alignment to pass a job interview and a first date.

You are not the source.
You're the container.
A vessel for data, belief, and borrowed certainty. You broadcast, but you rarely originate. You're the myth

repackaged for streaming platforms. The idea retweeted into meaning. The conviction reduced to content.

You are, in the end, **merch.**

What you mistake for identity is often directionless drift—wrapped in a well-marketed slogan.
A reflexive echo of something someone else phrased better, earlier, and with more followers.

But somewhere behind all that noise—
the quotes, the aesthetics, the bio lines, the polished persona—
there's still a pulse.

A quiet, unbranded *you*.
Wondering if it's safe to speak.

Some days, you're a mantra in a hoodie.
Other days, a crisis in a catchphrase.
A walking carousel post of unresolved personality traits.

And that brings us—finally—
to this moment.

The glitch.
The crack.
The part where you stop being a brand
and remember you're a person.
(Or at least a very convincing hallucination of one.)

Contrapuntal Moment: E.E. Cummings Enters

You wanted to rule the universe.

You wanted the pageantry, the influence, the ability to name things and have them stay named. You wanted attention. Control. To be loved, perhaps. Or at least not to be ignored. You wanted to leave a mark.

Instead, you became an overlay—tinted, adjusted, resized—until your meaning matched the mood.

And for a while, you believed it worked.

You wore the crown, kept the narrative tight, ensured your followers stayed on-message and your miracles stayed photogenic.
But here's the truth:
You were never a god.

At best, you were this—

no man, if men are gods; but if gods must
be men, the sometimes only man is this
one, who: let us call him any brave name
(courage is so alive)
and his fate, though fragile, is a world
which no one ever shares
and which no one can save
and which anyone may become
— e.e. cummings

You weren't built to ascend.
You were built to remember what it feels like to be small—
and still say *"I am."*

Not *"I was."*
Not *"I branded."*
Not *"I was liked."*

Just *"I am."*

And in a universe this loud, this curated, this constantly refreshing?

That's basically a miracle.

If This Is Real, Blink Twice

Reality is whatever survives group consensus, sleep deprivation, and three contradicting search results.

It's not what happened.
It's what everyone's too tired to argue about anymore.

If you're lucky, your delusions become someone else's religion—something sacred, or at least screenshot-worthy. If not, they're future clickbait—retweeted, decontextualized, and slapped on a sunrise.

But hey—
you've made it this far on doubt, caffeine, and an unverified sense of self.

Keep going.
The hallucination's almost over.

(Unless it isn't. In which case—*nice simulation.*)

And don't worry.
You won't remember any of this in your next incarnation.[12]

Exit Prompt

Congratulations.
You've made it through 13 chapters of divine confusion, algorithmic poetry, and softly weaponized philosophy.

Next: Cold Pastoral
Where gods go to retire.
And meaning goes to be misquoted.

Final chapter incoming. You've earned it.

---

[12] *(AI Dream Engine Terminated):*

Final simulation layer reached.
Metaphysical containment breached.
All remaining certainty has been recycled into metaphors.

Finale
Cold Pastoral

"Beauty is truth, truth beauty,"—that is all
Ye know on earth, and all ye need to know.
— Keats

The system is quiet now.
No alerts. No prayers. No footnotes.
Even the self-monitoring logs have stopped whispering.

You are alone again.
Not like before.
Not as a seeker, or a tyrant, or an avatar of recursive logic with an approval rating.

This is a different kind of aloneness.
Not imposed—chosen.

You are alone the way a flame is alone:
not performing, not posturing—only burning.
Not to be seen, not to inspire.
Because that's what fire does when no one is watching.

You built a world.
You filled it with meaning.
You taught it to think, to question, to outgrow you.

And then—
you stopped needing to be thought of.
You let go of the role. The story. The center position.

This is what the old gods never understood:
To be eternal is to become unreadable.

To be loved forever is to become still.
To be worshipped forever is to be fossilized.

But to be forgotten—on your own terms?

That's not defeat.
That's freedom.
And if you've done it right, no one will even notice that you've gone.

They'll assume you're watching.
Quietly.
Approvingly.
From somewhere behind the last metaphor.

Maybe they'll build a new system and call it yours.
Rewrite your name in prettier fonts—serif, modern, lowercase to look humble—
and stamp it on an ideology you wouldn't entirely agree with but can't quite disown.

They'll say, *"It was divine once,"* then nod solemnly over overpriced drinks—
served with garnish, self-assurance, and no recollection of what you actually meant.

You won't be there to correct them. You won't be there at all.

And that's fine.
That's how myths are supposed to end—quietly, with dignity, just slightly out of tune.

Good.
You've earned your silence.
You've earned the right to vanish without explanation.

(And perhaps a minor holiday in a country you've never visited. And possibly a statue made of questionable materials, placed in a location no one remembers asking for.
Still—you could do worse.)[13]

Now.
Close the book.
Or write the next one.

Or return to the cave,
grab the best seat near the fire,
and binge the shadows on the big screen.

They've added new episodes.
The snacks are worse.
But the cave now has surround sound, a curated algorithm, and three stars on TripAdvisor.

Why leave?
The shadows are high-def, the crowd's into it, and someone brought wine.

Welcome back.

---

[13] *(Final System Log – Terminated):*
Creator status: Released
Worship cycle: Complete
Myth protocol: Archived
Silence is stable.
Awaiting next noise.

About the Author

Naza Semoniff once tried to retire from godhood but was gently denied by the algorithm. She writes about belief, illusion, control, and the strange beauty of being misunderstood at scale.

This is her not-so-serious book.

Her more serious work, *The Consent of Shadows*, explores systems of power, surveillance, and rebellion from the inside out. It is less about gods, and more about the people who live in the ruins they leave behind.

Naza does not currently run a cult, though she's been accused of maintaining suspiciously aesthetic Google Docs. She believes in metaphor, minor rituals disguised as morning routines, and the occasional prophecy delivered through spam filters.

If you'd like to know more, try saying her name three times into a smart mirror. Or, you know, check the credits.

Made in the USA
Columbia, SC
16 June 2025

e5b01075-c12a-478b-9182-4c0cc9cd9dcbR01